♥ Praise for The Champion Advantage

— **Frank DeAngelis, Columbine High School Principal, 1996-2014, Author, They Call Me "Mr. De", The Story of Columbine's Heart, Resilience, and Recovery**

"An incredible book written by an extraordinary human being. The inspirational stories shared in this book will serve as motivation to make positive changes in one's life. As Hernani Alves, so eloquently states The Most Important Person Is You.

The book reminds us that we are never alone and that we are on the journey together during the good times and the unpredictable times. I have stated on numerous occasions you cannot determine what happens to you, but you can determine your response.

Hernani gives us the lessons to produce a positive response that can be life changing. As caring people, we are called upon to help others, especially during difficult times; but we cannot help others if we do not take care of ourselves.

I truly believe that we must not dwell on the negative in our lives but build upon the positive. Hernani gives us all the resources and knowledge to make changes in our lives and the lives of others.

The Acts of Kindness Chapter is advice that everyone would benefit from implementing. I would encourage you to read this incredible book; we need its message now more than ever.

Hernani is a true inspiration, and I'm honored to call him a colleague and more importantly, a friend." - **Frank DeAngelis**

♥

"This book will guide you through the importance of failure while achieving success. Hernani gives several examples on how to achieve thought provoking successes through tenacity and grit. I found this book very inspiring, and I can't wait to 'take actions' to achieve my successes."
— **Kelle Scott, Oklahoma State University, Program Manager with the Center for Executive and Professional Development at the Spears School of Business**

♥

"Hernani fills this book with the same inspiration and energy he brings to his life! From the first chapter to the last, I was captured by the stories and practical examples for making change. The book provides illustrations from some of the most successful leaders in history as well as amazing examples from Hernani's own life that help you see what's possible!"
— **Craig McAndrews, University of Houston, Professor of Practice, C.T. Bauer College of Business**

♥

"Hernani's first book was a powerful tool for me to relook at accountability and find better ways of driving it with my teams as well, growing their potential and productivity. This second book is much more focused on oneself, filled with tips and tools to help us win. And much like he advises, a key step to winning is never quitting, so don't quit now, stop finding excuses, read this book and find your Champion Advantage."

— **Eduardo Clemente, Executive Director, Standard Bank, Angola, Africa**

"Hernani uses authenticity in his storytelling to simplify concepts and ideas into something we can all achieve. His books have provided a way to inspire and unite my staff around a strong message of what it takes to be a Champion, both personally and professionally. I wholeheartedly recommend this book!"
— **Dee Ann Harn, CEO/Owner RFI Enterprises, Inc.**

"The champion mindset is a quick read with a mighty impact. It has quality concepts with easy to implement action steps for all positions in an organization. I personally worked alongside Hernani for decades, and he lives and breathes the concepts in the book, which has made a major impact on lives for the better."
— **Matt Anderson, Vice President, Inclusive Talent Solutions, PRIDE Industries**

"Hernani does a great job of weaving relatable stories with practical guidance. The Champion Advantage is a must-read for anyone who has ever felt uncertain or stuck, as it will arm you with the tools to change your mindset and create a more enriching path forward."
— **Tammy Dudek, Communications Strategist, Interact Software**

♥

"Once again, Hernani has demonstrated his unique ability to translate real life events into concrete workable business/life principles. The Champion Advantage cuts through complexity and identifies workable "take action" principles, practices and tools that help you navigate your mindset towards focused goals and positive outcomes. I can't wait to put my new learnings into practice!"

— **Sherif Tadros, Strategic Business Partner, BBSI**

♥

"For someone like me who is completely motivated by storytelling this is my perfect type of leadership book! Hernani weaves in personal stories, but then gives you this amazing detail into the lives of champions we all know and uses their stories to build a foundation that we can all use to succeed. This book is different from so many in that each chapter ends with thought provoking and action taking questions making this book truly experiential!"

— **Brett Thornton, Vice President of Retail and VX at Avocado and Host of the podcast "Just Stories with BT"**

The
CHAMPION
ADVANTAGE

Mastering How To WIN At Home and Work

HERNANI ALVES

Copyright © 2021 by Hernani Alves.

All rights reserved. No part of this publication may be reproduced, distributed, or transmitted in any form or by any means, including photocopying, recording, or other electronic or mechanical methods, without the prior written permission of the publisher, except in the case of brief quotations embodied in critical reviews and certain other noncommercial uses permitted by copyright law. For permission requests, write to the publisher, addressed "Attention: Permissions Coordinator," at the address below.

The Champion Advantage
Mastering the Mindset to Win at Home and Work
By Hernani Alves

Published by: Balanced IQ, LLC
8814 Fiador Court, Roseville, CA 95747, USA.
www.HernaniAlves.com
Cover Design: JDA Designs

Ordering Information:
Balanced IQ offers excellent discounts on this book when ordered in quantity for bulk purchases or special sales. For more information, please contact Hernani.Alves@BalancedIQ.com.

ISBN-13: 978-1-7337791-5-9   Hardback
ISBN-10: 1-7337791-5-9

ISBN-13: 978-1-7337791-6-6   Paperback
ISBN-10: 1-7337791-6-6

Library of Congress Cataloging-in-Publication Data
(hardback) 1. Belief and Doubt. 2. Success – (Psychology) 3. Motivation (Psychology).
I. Title

www.HernaniAlves.com

Email: Contact@BalancedIQ.com

To my siblings…

Fatima Madruga (Alves) for always showing me motherly love and giving me all the opportunity to succeed.

Joe Alves for keeping me in line and showing me how to maximize all the time you have on this beautiful earth.

Mario Alves for showing me you can always smile and laugh at what life has to offer.

Mike Alves for all our fun adventures and amazing friendship.

Love you all, Unconditional!

Contents

- [1] What's Important Now (W-I-N) 21
- [2] Failing Your Way to Success 31
- [3] A True Champion 39
- [4] The Most Important Person 47
- [5] A Fixed Mindset vs A Growth Mindset .. 55
- [6] Playing to Win 63
- [7] Positive Science 69
- [8] Brain Science 77
- [9] Body Science 85
- [10] Acts of Kindness 95
- [11] Celebrate your Success 105
- About the author 112
- Resources 113

"You're Braver Than YOU Believe,

Stronger Than You Seem And

Smarter Than You Think."

—Christopher Robin -"Pooh's Grand Adventure."

More than ever, we need to refocus and maximize what is important in our life at that very moment.

The leaders that maximize controllables and reset their lives will get a head start to winning like a Champion.

[1]

What's Important Now (W-I-N)

"If you continually ask yourself, What's Important Now (W-I-N)? You won't waste your time on the Trivial."

—Lou Holtz, University of Notre Dame Football Coach in the College Hall of Fame.

The world is feeling the adverse effects of stress, anxiety, and panic. We read about the stressful headlines every day: job loss, uncertainty, death tolls. It's not very motivating. The world is more of a negative place than it was even a few years ago, according to Gallup's Negative Experience Index. The index, a measure of people's experiences of stress, anger, sadness, physical pain, and worry, has crept upward.

In life, we encounter problems as often as we breathe. But they don't get to us until we feel a *major* challenge, and that's when the mounting problems become a source of concern, hurt, or sorrow. The three major pain areas in life that affect us right now are home life, work life, and how we feel about ourselves.

At home, there may not be anything more sweet than love and family life. As technology has improved to help us at home, it has also become a bigger distraction. Families are spending more time holding their phones and playing games or scrolling through their social media feed. A heavy dose of both has caused an increase in depression and loved ones are left fighting for more personal time together.

In your quest to become more successful at work, you've likely encountered animosity from toxic coworkers or managers. It may have been caused by differences in attitudes, unhealthy competition, or some undeserving colleague that gets all the credit over you.

These home and work challenges contribute to, and are affected by, how we feel about ourselves. We tend to be our biggest critic and say very negative things to ourselves.

"I'm not good enough."

"I can't do it."

"I hate my body."

"It's too hard."

"Why bother? I'm too old."

"I'm so stupid."

"I give up."

"I'm too weak."

How do we filter out the noise and overcome this adversity that piles on from home, work, and ourselves?

Ask yourself this one question: "What's Important Now?" Think W-I-N. Lou Holtz, the Hall of Fame football coach for the Notre Dame Football Team, used this strategy to motivate his players. He knew that he had these students during an interesting time in their lives. It was likely their first time away from home facing the many challenges and temptations of college life. Holtz used the W-I-N tool to help his players make better decisions during this exciting yet challenging time.

So how does Lou Holtz's concept of W-I-N translate during a time the world is becoming more negative? What's important now?

Well, right now, it's focusing on success and following the strategies in this book. How many times have you seen two different people experience the exact same event and have a totally different reaction to it? One person might get incredibly upset, while the other person not only isn't bothered by the experience, and actually enjoys it. One person might ask What's Important Now, and respond to that, while the other person might wallow in despair, frustration, and blame.

Responding with Focus

I've seen, first hand, what happens when you take a difficult experience and use it to focus on what's important in that moment. It was one of the most difficult times in my family's history. My father was a serial entrepreneur who taught me my first business—and life—lessons. He was born on the Azores Islands, which are located halfway between New York and Portugal. His island, Sao Jorge, was just 4 miles wide by 27 miles long, and there weren't many opportunities there. When Dad was only 18, he would look out over the water and think, *There must be more to life than this*.

It was the 1950s, and Angola, in southern Africa, was prospering with diamond mining. So Dad saved his money and persuaded a stranger to sell him their ticket for the fully-booked boat to Lobito, Angola. The journey took two months, and when Dad arrived, he had nowhere to go. There was no Google, no Yelp, and he didn't speak the language. He was homeless for two weeks and ate scrap food before finding a job at a trading post.

People would bring eggs, milk, whatever they had from their farm, and barter for what they needed. It was essentially a sales job, and dad became the top salesman. He loved it and, at 21 years old, summoned his courage and asked the owner to help him open his own store. The owner gave him a credit limit, and soon, the new store was up and running.

It Wasn't Easy

Dad would take anything as payment; quilts, pigs, chickens, whatever it took to sell something. But he never gave up. He met and married my mom, who joined him in the business. Over the years, they opened two trading posts, then two auto body shops, and an auto parts store. They went from poverty to the upper classes. They bought a big house, filled it with nice things, and lived a good life. They had my older sister, my two brothers, and, in June of 1975, my mom gave birth to me.

That year, 1975, is burned into the collective memory of all Angolans. It was the year the civil war started. No one knew it then, but that war would last 27 years and take the lives of more than five hundred thousand people. Over one million people would be displaced, and we were to be among them.

Losing Everything

I was three months old when it happened. It was early morning. Mom was preparing breakfast, and there was a knock on the door of the house like you've never heard. It was a knock to scare you. It happened again. It was loud. It was aggressive. Dad thought, *Is this a threat? Do I open the door?*

He took a chance, unlocked the door, and peered out. The neighbor stood on the doorstep, looking frantic. He shouted at my dad, "Get out! Get out! The guerrilla army is coming. They're going to kill you. Leave now." My dad grabbed the kids, his wife, and a bottle of milk for the baby—me, and got out of there.

He and my mom found a Red Cross refugee camp in South Africa. Thank God for the Red Cross. But it was tough there. It was overpopulated. People would fight for bread and scavenge scraps of food from the dirt to feed their kids. Our family survived, and after six months, we were able to escape. A lot of people didn't. Some had so much stress they had heart attacks. Others couldn't deal with everything they'd lost, and took their own lives.

Finding Success, Again

My parents had lost everything, too. However, being the entrepreneur he was, dad started again. Back in the Azores Islands, he opened a restaurant. He did well but still wanted a better life for his children. He brought us to the beautiful United States, started that fish market, then the dairy farm, and provided comfort and countless opportunities for me, my sister, and my brothers, including my younger brother who was born in the United States.

I grew up hearing this story, and it gave me profound confidence that success is possible for anyone, in any circumstances. If you focus on what's important in any given moment, you can be successful in the areas of life that matter. So when I was 23 and got a part-time job for a mattress retailer in California called Sleep Train, I assumed I would be successful there. To my surprise, after growing with the company in different leadership roles for 15 years,

I was appointed President, and we evolved into a brand worth over $3 billion, with over 3,500 locations throughout the United States, and more than 15,000 fantastic employees. I loved my work, and I loved the people I worked with. My success was due to the people I worked with—a high-performing team who taught me the power of mental toughness. Their wisdom, experience, and honesty helped me learn the lessons I'll share with you in this book.

Make a Commitment to W-I-N

I want you to make a commitment to yourself. You're reading this book because things aren't as good as they could be in your life, but you want it to improve. You're in a difficult situation, managing multiple tasks, with constant challenges being thrown at you. It isn't easy.

Using the processes you'll learn in this book, you can turn things around. In these pages, you'll discover how to succeed with confidence, who the most important person in your world is (the answer might surprise you), the difference between a fixed mindset and a growth one—and what that means when we compare bison to cows. You'll learn how to play to win, and what positive science, brain science, and body can do for your business. You'll see the importance of acts of kindness and celebrating successes.

We'll end each chapter with a few questions to ask yourself, and some action items so you can take solid steps toward your goal of a well-functioning workplace. You can keep your answers private or share them with me at Hernani@BalancedIQ.com. I'd love to hear how you're doing and be by your side.

If you follow the action items, you'll see real changes in your life. You and your team will perform better and see more success than ever before. In turn, you'll have less stress, feel more accomplished, and give those same benefits to others.

So commit to reading this book all the way through and acting on its advice. It's all tested, proven action that will make a difference in your life. You won't have to do this alone; I'll guide you through each step. You do have to take action, though.

You should, right? You owe it to yourself to try. I live my life by Albert Einstein's famous quote, "Insanity is doing the same thing, over and over again, but expecting different results." It's time to change the game plan.

It's time to W-I-N!

✓ Take Action

- ✓ Commit to reading this book all the way through and acting on its advice.

- ✓ List the top three things that are causing you stress and anxiety in your life.

- ✓ Ask yourself, "In life, What's Important Now? And at work, What's Important Now?" Write down your answers.

- ✓ Let's be Friends. Please follow me at:
  LinkedIn.com/in/Hernani-Alves

♥

Hernani's new book "The Champion Advantage" is the springboard to propel his readers into developing a better version of themselves. He shares how everything starts with our attitude, mindsets and reminds us of the importance of self-care and kindness.

The questions following each chapter provide a personal blueprint for the reader to put their plans into action. I hope every reader realizes it is never too late to change and is willing to learn how to make a positive difference in life, spread kindness, choose growth, and agree with Hernani's mantra, "doing nothing should never be an option!"

— **Dana Almora – Corporate Training Director - PRIDE Industries**

♥

[2]

Failing Your Way To Success

> **"Do not judge me by my successes; judge me by how many times I fell down and got back up again."**
>
> —Nelson Mandela, former President of South Africa and world philanthropist.

Let's face it; no one enjoys the feeling of failing. Especially if you've put a lot of time and effort into something, failing never feels good. However, not succeeding at first teaches you a lot about yourself and how to survive. One of the most essential qualities of becoming successful is the determination to never give up.

Keep Your Focus

One inspirational story of not giving up is that of Nelson Mandela. He was born in 1918 in South Africa. As the foster son of a Thembu chief, he grew up impoverished, but quickly set his sights on fighting discrimination on the grounds of race. While he was initially against acts of violence, a massacre of black, unarmed South Africans in 1962 changed his mind, and he started to advocate for sabotage against the oppressive government. After an arrest and an eventual trial in 1964, Mandela received a life prison sentence.

Mandela wasn't forgotten while he was locked up. Instead, he became symbolic of the anti-apartheid movement across the world. Several times, the authorities offered to release Mandela if he would reverse his support of violent protesting. Each time, he refused. He was eventually released in 1990 as a hero. Just three years later, in South Africa's first ever election that allowed residents of all races to vote, Mandela was elected. During his presidency, he fought for the reconciliation of all races.

Mandela's survival of 27 years in prison while maintaining a constant focus on human rights is inspiring. It would be challenging to last that long in prison. Not only did he do that, but after his exit, he went on to be the oldest elected President of South Africa, at 75 years old.

8 Secrets of Success

Mandela's focus and perseverance are reminiscent of Richard St. John's '8 Secrets of Success.' St. John is a self-described average guy who found success doing what he loved. He spent more than a decade researching the lessons of success. He conducted over one thousand face-to-face interviews with many of the world's most successful people, including Bill Gates, Richard Branson, the Google founders, Rupert Murdoch, and the list goes on. From there, he developed 8 Secrets to Success:

1. **Passion** - Do what you do for love, not money.

2. **Work** - Work hard and have fun working.

3. **Good** - Practice until you are good at what you do.

4. **Focus** - Keep your eye on one thing.

5. **Push yourself** - Push yourself physically and mentally, through shyness and self-doubt.

6. **Serve** - Successful people serve others something of value.

7. **Ideas** - Listen, observe, be curious, ask questions, problem solve, and make connections.

8. **Persist** - Keep going through failure, criticism, rejection, difficult people, and pressure.

Just look around and you'll see many examples of these qualities in people who have succeeded in our culture. And many of them had to fail first in order to find their success.

If you think about it, failing is succeeding. The faster you can fail, the quicker you will succeed. When you fail, you can learn from your mistakes and then do something differently.

Albert Einstein is widely credited with the famous saying, "The definition of insanity is doing the same thing over and over again but expecting different results." Most people know Einstein successfully developed the Theory of Relativity (even if they, like me, don't really understand it). He had many more famous successes—and even you may not have heard were his. Einstein's inventions helped create paper towels, lasers, stock market forecasts, and solar power.

Walt Disney Believed in a Dream

One success story that first met failure head-on was that of Walt Disney. He first dropped out of school and then tried—and failed—to join the army. One of his early companies, Laugh-o-Gram Studios, didn't succeed and went bankrupt because he just didn't understand how to run a business.

Disney was even fired from a newspaper job because he was "not creative enough." Through his perseverance, Walt Disney is now a household name and responsible for movies and theme parks that will be enjoyed for countless decades to come.

Defeat after defeat, Walt Disney kept trying. Failure is really just a success in progress. If you continually avoid failure, you'll probably never succeed. Success comes from moments of frustrations when you're the most uncomfortable. After you've gone through all the bitter times, you'll be more robust, which will propel you closer to success.

Smart After All

Another example of failing to succeed is the story of Richard Branson, the founder of Virgin Group, which controls more than four hundred companies world-wide. To start, Branson was not a successful student. He said, "I was seen as the dumbest person at school. The idea that I could be successful didn't dawn on me." He suffered from dyslexia. This caused his grades to fail and his passions to grow.

He started a magazine called "Student," which wasn't very successful itself but led to a profit-making mail-order discount record business. This eventually inspired him to open his first record store, and then led to his own record label. Today, he's known around the world for his connection to Virgin Records, and the entire Virgin Brand that puts over seventy thousand people to work.

Virgin isn't Branson's only business. He created 12 other billion-dollar companies and was named one of the most influential people in the world in 2007. By 2017, he had built his net worth to over $5 billion and, in his spare time, authored several books. When you look back at the student who was considered the least successful in his school, his eventual achievements are astounding.

We Can All Keep Going

We are all able to have a success story like that of Richard Branson. He found his passions and kept trying ventures that led to new ventures, each one building on the success—or failure—of the other. He didn't give up.

For many people who end up being successful, quitting isn't an option. And neither is allowing themselves to fear failure. Don't be afraid to fail. In fact, get on the road and start failing. And fail often. The lessons you learn will put you on the path to your own success. Nelson Mandela has inspired the world with one statement in particular. He said, "Judge me by how many times I fell down and got back up again."

✓ Take Action

- ✓ Is there a dream that you've always had, but the fear of failure holds you back? If so, write it down.

- ✓ Write down some ways you can limit the risk of failure in pursuing your dream.

- ✓ Write out the top three personal habits you've been wanting to develop to become the person who could succeed at this dream.

♥

"The Champion Advantage is a must read for any leader looking to be more impactful in all realms of their life. The intentionality to Take Action at the end of each chapter is uniquely Hernani and one that empowers you to see progress and growth as you read."
— **Cameron Law, California State University, Sacramento, Executive Director of the Carlsen Center for Innovation & Entrepreneurship**

♥

[3]

A True Champion

> **"In our lives, we have to stand up for what is right, even though we are standing alone."**
>
> —Frank DeAngelis, Principal, Columbine High School 1996 - 2014, a national treasure who has transformed the school safety conversation world-wide.

There are always going to be moments of crisis in business and in life. However, it is not the event that defines you as a leader, but how you react to the event. Roman Emperor Marcus Aurelius once said, "You have the power over your mind- not the outside events. Realize this, and you will find strength." Those same words still hold true today.

When the chips are down, and your worst fear becomes your reality, what separates good leaders from great leaders is your mindset. Having that champion mindset is how you cope with adversity.

It started as a typical school day in Littleton, Colorado, on April 20, 1999. I can still clearly recall the images of Columbine High School. For me, it was the first time I had witnessed such horror in our sacred schools. On an otherwise typical day, two shooters opened fire on their classmates, killing 12 students and one teacher. Frank DeAngelis was the principal at that time, and from that event, he emerged as a true champion leader for so many.

From that day on, Frank's life, his student's lives, and every child in American schools were forever changed. As a leader, people look to Frank on how to recover and overcome such a tragedy. His response and resilience are now relied upon by school officials across the country.

In an interview, I had the opportunity to ask Frank how a person overcomes such a tragedy. According to Frank, every event in life shapes our way of thinking. For a person to overcome a setback, they must have the right mindset. It is how you keep going. You have to learn from the experience and find something positive from it.

During a crisis moment, that's when a leader's character and abilities are put to the test. Over twenty years later, Frank is still recalling his painful experience of that day and still learning from it. For him and all leaders, dealing with adversity makes you stronger and better. His faith in finding solutions and a positive mindset about the future is what guides Frank in his ability to carry on.

What is a real champion?

If we take Frank's life as a blueprint, it centers on humility—but also so much more. Let's start with a little more about Frank himself.

Frank was first a teacher at Columbine before he was promoted to principal. After that fated day in 1999, he made a promise to himself that he would stay principal of Columbine until every student who had experienced that tragedy firsthand had graduated.

As the years went on, he extended his stay until every young student in the Columbine area who even witnessed the tragedy on television graduated as well. He is known in the community for "persevering for a cause greater than himself." He rose to the occasion for which he was uniquely called.

Even after Frank retired, he continued to mentor other principals and their communities that experienced school shootings. As horrible as that day and how unwelcome the experience, Frank believes, "Columbine offers hope." And he feels chosen to give that hope.

What can we learn from Frank's life about being a true champion?

Frank rose to the call. He is not a stranger to responding to a calling. As a very serious young person, he was drawn to be an educator. He was so devoted that his own principal once took his school keys away from him, demanding that he take the weekend off. As a teacher, his students remember his motto in life. They reported him saying to them, "Be a good student, be a good athlete, but above all else, be a good person."

Frank is a true champion leader. When the shootings happened, there were those in the community that felt like the world had lost faith in them, in their school. But Frank was a believer in Columbine and led them out of that darkness. Even after that dark day in 1999, his focus on leadership was one not based on fear. He didn't want his students to fear him so they would respect him, and as a coach, he taught his players, "You have to motivate your players and play with the hand you're dealt."

He is astute in how he handles people and getting them to see other people's viewpoints. He always portrayed a "one of us" attitude and tried to understand where people are coming from. As a principal, he would switch jobs with teachers to role play and see things from other people's shoes. He believes that leadership is a combination of getting input and being flexible.

Frank gives back. He continues to be sought after by others dealing with the same events he did—after the Columbine tragedy, he stated, "I just joined a club in which no one wants to become a member." Frank continues to teach in his own way, giving presentations about the recovery process he's experienced. He also spends his time serving on boards focused on school safety.

Frank is human. He has skills gained from counseling, such as two medals he wears around his neck. When reminded of that dark day, he rubs these two medals and says to himself, "This is not April 20, 1999; this is (today's date.)" He has to remind himself sometimes that he is safe. Many see him as a hero, but to Frank, he is just a man with some transformative mottos for life.

A True Champion Believes:
- People don't care how much you know until they know how much you care.
- Every day may not be good, but there is good in every day. – *Alice Earle*
- Look for energy givers, not energy takers.
- Surround yourself with good people and then motivate them.
- It's the little things that make a big difference.

- Don't dwell on the negative; maximize the positive.

It is easy to see why Frank emerged from a tragic event as a true champion with that kind of attitude.

Those who know Frank well say he was transformed by the events of April 20, 1999, but it didn't turn him into a completely different person. Who he was at his core showed itself during the tragedy. And arguably, that may have been what held his school and community together.
The event changed him immensely. Every morning when he wakes up, he recites the name of the "Beloved 13." He remembers them in everything he does. He didn't panic during the tragedy and saved many students who were in the line of fire.

Failure is inevitable, but it is not permanent. Frank's tenacity is something that can be admired, and his story is one that inspires him to be there for those they serve.

As a leader, you must accept the reality of the situation, and like Frank, have the faith and the mindset that the situation will get better.

✓ Take Action

- ✓ Is there something in your life that you may be dwelling on the negative? If so, what is in detail?

- ✓ This will be difficult and hard to do: Is there anything positive that you learned from that difficult situation.

- ✓ Frank's focus is looking for energy givers, not energy takers. Are there any energy takers that you need to avoid?

♥

"The inspirational stories shared in this book will serve as motivation to make positive changes in one's life. As Hernani Alves, so eloquently states The Most Important Person Is You."

— **Frank DeAngelis, Columbine High School Principal, 1996-2014, Author, They Call Me "Mr. De", The Story of Columbine's Heart, Resilience, and Recovery**

♥

[4]

The Most Important Person

> **"Just believe in yourself. Even if you don't, pretend that you do and at some point, you will."**
>
> — Venus Williams, champion women's tennis player, and four-time Olympic gold medalist.

In chapter 1, we started by asking ourselves the question, "What's Important Now?" You are reading this book, so I can confidently guess that things are challenging for you at the moment. No one is perfect in this world, and you are either getting better or worse. There is no middle ground; it's either better or worse. As my old college soccer coach would say, "There's always room for improvement."

When things aren't going right in your life, you have to decide if you will take the hit. Sure, there may be legitimate reasons outside of your control for why you're facing particular challenges. But some of the negative stuff in your life may be your fault; maybe you misjudged an action.

Taking the hit means you accept responsibility for your life. You acknowledge that you have the power to control your world, or at least the way you respond to it. It means you understand that *your* actions—or inaction—have led to your current situation. This isn't about blame; it's about accepting responsibility.

So, will you take the hit?

Now is the time to decide. As that wise, old transformer, Optimus Prime, said in *Transformers: Age of Extinction*, "Often, the most important moments in life come to this exact moment. What are you going to do?"

Choosing to take the hit is essential. As we move through the book, you'll see it's the foundation for all your future success. I'll give you a moment to make your decision.

Excuses: The Language of Losers

If you decided to take the hit, congratulations! That's a big deal. You're on the way to real change. You see, when you choose to take the hit, you stop making excuses. Excuses are the language of losers. This idea was drilled into me when I was nine-years-old, playing in my first ever soccer season.

When we lived in Idaho, we'd occasionally get bad weather toward the end of the soccer season. In one of my first playoff games with the team, it snowed. It wasn't that fun, fluffy stuff; it was cold, wet, heavy snowflakes driving down onto the slippery field.

At half-time, we were losing 3-0. Our coach wasn't happy. He gathered us around and asked, "What's going on? You're getting your butts kicked out there." Us kids looked at each other and didn't say a word. He asked again, "What is it? Why are you playing so timid? You're better than this."

After a long moment, I decided I'd tell him. "We don't play well when it's snowing. The field sucks. And it's cold." Coach looked at me with disgust and said, "Are you kidding me? You're playing in the same weather, on the same field, as the other team. No more excuses."

It was brilliant. That one statement shut down all our excuses. We went out there and won the game. I don't remember the end score, but I do remember how empowered we felt in that second half.

After that, we actually wanted to play in bad weather. We knew the sleet and snow would get to the other teams, but we wouldn't let it stop us. Instead of whining about the cold, we focused on what we could control on the field. We went on to have a fantastic winning streak.

Are you Making Excuses?

Have you been making excuses in your game? It's human nature to look for someone or something else to blame. No one is perfect. We are humans. We make mistakes. We make excuses, which are a part of a victim mentality.

Victim mentality is when we don't think about solutions but dwell on what went wrong, and whose fault it was, and all the reasons we're not to blame.

Of course, there's a time and place for considering what went sideways in a situation, or who should take the fall. But with a hero mentality, we ditch the excuses and focus on solutions first. With a victim mentality, we wallow in how unfair it all is and how powerless we are.

If your natural instinct is to fall into a victim mindset, you should know this is a normal part of being human. However, it's something you must address if you want to achieve greatness.

It's not easy to ditch the victim mentality, particularly if it's become a habit for you. It's also hard when horrible things happen to us. That's life. There will be people who let us down, someone who cuts us off, accidents that occur, bills that don't get paid, and the deaths of special people in our lives.

You First

As a business consultant, when I first meet with the company's leadership team, it is usually in a boardroom. I'll ask them, "Who is the most important person in the world to you?"

The answers are what you'd expect. It's usually, my mom, my wife, my husband, my kids. Then, I ask again. They're intelligent folks, so they know I'm fishing for a different answer. After a pause, they figure it out.

The most important person in the world is themselves.

Think of when the flight attendant says to put your own oxygen mask on first. You can't get your child out of the plane if you're passed out on the seat beside him because you were too busy fixing their mask first.

Next, I ask, "What do you control about yourself?" The answer is: everything. This isn't rocket science, but it gives those busy, stressed-out executives a moment to reflect, and remember that they control themselves.

This is a good reminder for all of us. It's a reality check that reveals it's not everyone else's fault when you're not getting the results you want. You can't control the world, but you can take charge of your own actions.

Take a moment to consider how this sits with you. Do you find it empowering? Does it overwhelm you? Maybe there's a bit of both going on. These ideas may even bring forth some guilt when you realize you could've taken control of a situation from the beginning.

It's okay. Don't let that guilt get to you.

Life is one long learning process. Michelangelo, a famous Italian painter, was 87 years old when he said, "I am still learning." This was the man who painted the Sistine Chapel in his mid-thirties!

It sounds counter-intuitive, but when you learn to look after yourself first, you will do better—for you and everyone around you. The great news is that we'll work on this together for the rest of the book.

✓ Take Action

- ✓ What are some things that you neglect to do for yourself?

- ✓ What excuses have you been making about yourself? Write them down.

- ✓ Write down what it looks like for you to take the hit, accept responsibility, and make improvements to get what you want.

- ✓ Now answer this great question: What do you really want?

♥

"Having read Hernani's first book, *Balanced Accountability*, I was super excited to hear about his second book and he did not disappoint! The Champion Advantage does a great job of using Hernani's personal experiences in the business world to remind the reader of many fundamental business principles. As a business owner I found the book to be very useful."

— **John Palley, California Probate Attorney**

♥

[5]

A Fixed Mindset Versus A Growth Mindset

> "Change can be tough, but I've never heard anybody say it wasn't worth it."
>
> —Dr. Carol Dweck, Professor of Psychology at Stanford University.

Dr. Carol Dweck, Professor of Psychology at Stanford University, studies human motivation. She spends her days diving into why people succeed (or don't) and what's within our control to foster success. Her theory of the two mindsets and the difference they make in outcomes is a great study. Having a Fixed or a Growth Mindset affects more than you think. Simply put, when you have a Fixed Mindset, you believe that you were born with your current abilities, and you aren't able to change them. However, when you have a Growth Mindset, you can maximize all the things within your control to improve your abilities through practice.

Think of two young kids who love basketball, but neither of them is very good at it. The kid with a Fixed Mindset won't even try out or practice shooting baskets every night to try to improve his game. He'll think he wasn't born with the natural ability.

On the other hand, the kid with a Growth Mindset will practice before and after school; he'll ask the coach to give him more pointers, he'll watch great players, eat well and gear up for tryouts. Whether or not he makes the team, he still has a Growth Mindset.

Feedback Opportunity

People with a Fixed Mindset also see failure as a dead end and take criticism personally. Conversely, someone with a Growth Mindset considers failure as a chance to find a new way of doing things. Growth Mindset also sees feedback in the same way—as an opportunity to make improvements and create new systems.

Someone with a Fixed Mindset is likely to think, "Why even try?" They tend to take the easy way out and put in the minimally-required effort. Growth Mindset seeks out challenges and embraces them. When someone with a Fixed Mindset encounters an obstacle, they are more likely to give up, and they like accomplishments that can be measured, like good grades. Growth Mindsets seek continuous improvement and feel it's never too late to learn something new.

Dr. Dweck noticed this same phenomenon in what she called "The Power of Yet." She worked with Chicagoan students who were given a "not yet" instead of a "fail" when they didn't pass their class. This gave Dr. Dweck a path into her future.

A turning point in her career came when she worked with a group of 10-year-olds. They were given tasks a little beyond their capabilities to observe how they coped with the challenges. For some of the students, they declared, "I like a challenge!" They had the Growth Mindset. They believed their abilities could be developed beyond where they currently were.

However, some other students were upset. They felt like they were being judged by their lack of intelligence because they couldn't complete the tasks. Dr. Dweck said, "Instead of luxuriating in the power of yet, they were gripped in the tyranny of now."

Brain Fire

People with a Growth Mindset approach failure differently. Someone with a Fixed Mindset is more likely to cheat the next time they try a task, while someone with a Growth Mindset will concentrate on studying more. If you have a Fixed Mindset, you may find yourself looking for people who are doing worse than you are so you see yourself in a better light. If you're Fixed, you also tend to run from difficult situations. When you're in Growth, you engage more deeply, and your "brain is on fire with yet," according to Dr. Dweck.

Work to change your mindset and move out of your comfort zone. Every time you do, you learn something new, and this forces your brain neurons to make new connections. In other words, you get smarter.

Interestingly, Dr. Dweck found that the power of yet also creates equality in our learning systems. When implementing these strategies, generally underperforming populations like inner cities and Native American reservations excelled. She explained that change and improvement evolved because "the meaning of effort and difficulty was transformed."

The Bison Versus The Cow

You can see this same phenomenon in the animal world. Take the bison and the cow. In the animal world, the cow has a Fixed Mindset. If cows see a storm coming, they'll run in the opposite direction. Trust me—I grew up on a dairy farm! The problem is that cows usually aren't fast enough to get away and they only delay their exposure to the storm for a short time as it catches up to them.

On the other hand, when bison see a storm coming, they run straight into it. Their Growth Mindset is to face it head-on and get the hard part over with, knowing that for them, the storm will then pass more quickly.

There are three questions I want you to ask yourself when you see a challenge coming:

1. What steps can I take to improve this challenge?
2. In what ways can I succeed through this challenge?
3. Which resources can I embrace to get through this challenge?

Notice that all of these questions involve "I," which means that no one else is responsible for your success. This will help you push your way through any challenge quickly.

Neuroplasticity

Here's an important fact: No matter how old you are, your brain has the ability to change. It's scientifically proven and it's called neuroplasticity. It allows you to make adjustments when you are faced with new situations throughout life.

If you are aware that your brain is constantly changing, then you are more likely to adopt a Growth Mindset. Remember that if the brain is not Fixed, then the mind should not be Fixed, either. We've all encountered those individuals who say, "I am who I am and I can't change." Neuroplasticity, in fact, contradicts their statement. They can become who they want to become.

My dad had a Growth Mindset. He sought out a better life when he left the Azores Island for Angola as a young man. And when there was a civil war, he picked himself and his family up and rebuilt his life to something bigger than before. He wasn't defeated when the situation became more than he thought he could handle. Many times, my dad told me, "The worst thing you can ever do is nothing."

Doing nothing means accepting negativity. The thing about negativity is that it's widespread and, worst yet, highly contagious. As such, negative thoughts tend to enter your mind. You're bound to encounter people who disagree with you or seem out to bring you down. Then there's the negative state of the world, where bad things happen to good people and innocent people suffer for no reason.

It is not easy to deal with the challenges you're having at work, at home, or in the world. If you can shift your thinking from a Fixed Mindset to a Growth Mindset, you're less likely to feel defeated by what you are facing. You may even evolve to see this time as a period of expansion and deeper meaning.

Let's continue on this journey as we think more about how we can have a *Champion* Growth Mindset. It's not a fast-track to success; it takes effort to train yourself to use a more productive mindset. As Dr. Dweck said, "Change can be tough, but I've never heard anybody say it wasn't worth it." She makes a great point and one that requires us to take action.

✓ Take Action

- ✓ Make notes about how you currently respond to problems. Do you have a Fixed or Growth Mindset? Why?

- ✓ List three things that are regularly on your mind, yet you've avoided taking action on.

- ✓ Review the What's Important Now that you identified in the last chapter. What are two Growth Mindset ideas you can implement to get your W-I-N?

- ✓ If you haven't done so already, let's stay in touch. I'm always by your side.

    Please follow me on LinkedIN, at:

    LinkedIn.com/in/Hernani-Alves

♥

"The concepts introduced in The Champion Advantage are thoughtful and well supported, but delivered with such simplicity. There are so many gems throughout the book that have forever changed my way of thinking."
— **Chris Gross, Director of Human Resources, Advanced Helicopter Services**

♥

[6]

Playing to Win

"I play to win, whether during practice or a real game."

— Michael Jordan, former National Basketball Player with Six Championships, and Most Valuable Player (MVP) Awards.

When you are thinking about having a Fixed Mindset versus a Growth Mindset, you also must have to consider if you're playing to win versus playing not to lose.

There's a subtle difference between playing to win and playing not to lose. However, you never win when you play not to lose. Why? Because you're focusing on what you *don't* want to happen.

Think about a skier learning to ski. They don't want to fall, right? Makes sense. Except in doing so, they overcompensate and then lean backward too much in an attempt not to fall forward. What does that cause them to do? Fall backward, of course. In a sense, they are playing not to lose, and that leads to precisely what they are trying to avoid.

Businesses do this, too. When sales are slowing down and things are getting tight, many companies will then start to cut back, when this is the exact time they should increase marketing and try outside-the-box tactics. They go into playing not to lose, and all of a sudden, they wonder what happened when sales dry up.

Imagine a fan blowing at high speed. Someone suddenly turns off its power. What happens? The fan continues to hum along, and after every revolution, it slows down. The fan eventually stops—until someone gives it energy again.

Unfortunately, a sports example of this is from my favorite team, the San Francisco 49ers. In the 2020 Super Bowl, the 49ers had a 20-10 lead against the Kansas City Chiefs with only seven minutes left on the clock. Instead of playing to win, the 49ers started to play not to lose. They played defensively, rather than offensively, and allowed the Chiefs to score 21 straight, unanswered points. This was a disappointing 20-31 loss—that is, if you're a 49ers fan. Yes, I'm still bitter about it.

Failing Fast Leads to Success

The great Michael Jordan and the Chicago Bulls are a perfect example of playing to win. In fact, Michael Jordan has been playing to win from a very young age. Some don't realize that he didn't even make his high school's varsity team his sophomore year.

Although he was always a good athlete, he was only 5'10" at the time, and there were already eight guards on their varsity team. It's hard to believe someone would cut Jordan from a basketball team, but at the time, he hadn't lived up to his name yet. Instead, they called him "Peanut" and were always making fun of him for his size. He just didn't stand out as anything special at first.

Although Jordan was crushed when he didn't make the team, he used the disappointment as motivation to improve his game. He worked on his defense and his shot, and when tryouts came the next year, he got in. He went on to average 25 points per game for his varsity team, and the name Jordan began to form the meaning it has today.

Even as a young man, Jordan learned something about his emotions from this experience. He discovered that in the pain, there was a lesson. He didn't like the pain he experienced by not achieving his goals. So, he turned his negative emotions into positive motivation and worked even harder. This work paid off for his team too, and the Chicago Bulls won six NBA championships during Jordan's tenure.

Throughout the Chicago Bulls' history, teams played not to lose to them, even though they first scored a lot of points against them. For instance, in the 1992 NBA championship finals, the Chicago Bulls trailed the Portland Trail Blazers by 13 points when the fourth quarter began. With Jordan sitting on the bench for the rally, Scottie Pippen and four bench players brought the Bulls back quickly.

With the Bulls back in the game, Jordan returned and notched two steals. Jordan scored a game-high 33 points. The Game 6 win closed the series for the Bulls, giving them their second straight championship.

The Bulls went on to win several more championships with the same mentality. They played to win. Their opponents played not to lose. And this is about individuals as much as it's about teams. Up until his final shot in the NBA, Michael Jordan played to win every single game.

Playing to Win Is A Growth Mindset

When you have this playing to win mindset, you believe your current situation is changeable. Just like Michael Jordan's story of not making his first varsity basketball team. We wouldn't have his great story or legacy if he were playing not to lose and thought he couldn't improve or grow to be arguably the greatest basketball player of all time.

✓ Take Action

- ✓ How about you? Are you currently playing to win or play not to lose? Write down your thoughts about this.

- ✓ List out the areas of your life in which you may be playing not to lose.

- ✓ Brainstorm three things you can do to add some energy to playing to win.

♥

"The Champion Advantage is written in a simple, to the point format, that helps readers understand what is important now and how to develop a growth mindset in your life. Highly recommend to anyone who wants to play to WIN."

— **Mike Laney, Director of Sales, Serta Simmons Bedding**

♥

[7]

Positive Science

> "That wall is your mind playing tricks on you. You just need to say, 'One more step. I can do this. I have more in me."
>
> —Kerry Walsh, professional beach volleyball player and three-time Olympic gold medalist.

You hear a lot in the media about being positive and how it's a good thing. It may sound like a lot of fluff, but there's real science behind the power of positivity.

Consider the story of my father going against the struggle of a civil war and the resulting economic fallout, only to build more and more businesses. My father had a positive attitude, and it propelled him through difficult times. But, there's more to the concept of positivity than meets the eye.

Positive thinking involves more than just thinking happy thoughts or having a good attitude. Instead, consider how positive thoughts create true value in your life. And how they build skills that help you through your life. It's helpful first to think about what negative and positive thoughts do and how your body reacts to them.

The World of Possibilities

Let's talk about what happens when you have a negative thought. Barbara Fredrickson, a researcher of positive psychology from the University of North Carolina, learned a lot about the impact from a paper she published.

She discovered that negative emotions narrow your mind and focus. They make you feel like your options are fewer than if you have positive thoughts. There are some very primal reasons for this.

Pretend you're on a walk and a tiger crosses your path. Your focus becomes narrow. Your drive is about how to get out of there with all your limbs. Your focus is on survival. Fear becomes your primary instinct. Any option other than fleeing seems irrelevant. (And in this situation, it probably is.)

This is actually a useful instinct. If you're trying to survive, other options are not helpful. Only the ones that will get you out of there—and fast—are going to be of any good.

Yet, we don't just have negative thoughts when we're at risk of being eaten by a tiger. For many people, negative thoughts are a regular occurrence. And they cut off the outside world, narrowing the options you see possible for yourself and your life.

Here's a practical example: Imagine you have a tremendously long to-do list for the day. If you are overwhelmed by the length of the list and have negative thoughts about it, you might feel paralyzed and not get anything done. It might keep you from even getting started.

The "Broaden and Build" Theory

A study was once conducted using five control groups. Each one was shown a film clip that either exhibited joy, contentment, fear, anger, or something neutral. After watching the clip, each group was asked to think about what they would do in a similar situation.

The joy and contentment groups came up with more possibilities regarding what they would do. They were open to more options, just as the positive thinking theories indicate.

This is based on the "broaden and build" theory. It says that positive emotions open your mind, which then allows you to build new skills and resources. Why do negative thoughts and feelings limit you? Because in a negative situation, when there is an immediate threat to your well-being, building skills is irrelevant.

So, how do you cultivate positive emotions and thoughts, so you can build new skills? According to an article by HuffPost, it involves focusing on "anything that sparks feelings of joy, contentment, and love." It also includes meditation, writing about positive experiences, and scheduling time for play and adventure. The article continues, "Happiness is essential to building the skills that allow for success."

The Loss Versus Gain Frame

Dr. Alison Ledgerwood is a social psychologist interested in how positive and negative thinking affects our outlook. Her studies have taught her that if someone focuses on the loss in a situation more than the gains, the outcome appears negative, and this negativity sticks with them.

For example, she presented a situation to two separate groups. To the first group, she talked about a type of surgery that has a seventy percent success rate. To another group, she talked in the same way about the same surgery, but she reversed the statistic. She said it had a thirty percent failure rate. Same surgery. Same presentation. Just a different way of presenting the statistic.

To the first group, where the surgery was presented in a positive light and in terms of gains, the procedure was viewed favorably. To the second group, where the surgery was presented in a negative light and in terms of losses, the surgical procedure was not seen as a good idea. Dr. Ledgerwood then told these two groups to look at the statistic in the opposite way. To those who were presented with a thirty percent failure rate, she reminded them that this meant there was a seventy percent chance of success, and vice versa. It didn't matter. Once the participants were presented with the negative, they couldn't see the positive anymore.

Ledgerwood took from these examples that our view of the world "tends to tilt toward the negative. We have to work harder to see the upside." She came up with three ways to change this.

1. **Rehearse good news**. When you come home from work and talk about your day, spend little time on the negative. Purposely find something positive that happened and talk about that.
2. **Focus on the upside in the community**. Counter the negative. For example, if you have a grumpy waiter, leave them a bigger tip than you feel he earned.
3. **Make a habit of writing down what you're grateful for in life**. It's so easy to overlook the amazing things we have in our lives that we would never trade away.

The Importance of Gratitude

Harvard researcher and author Shawn Achor has a few insights on gratitude. He said that doing something as simple as writing down three things you're grateful for over 21 days increases optimism and maintains it for the next six months.

He found gratitude also increases willpower and calmness, and boosts employee morale. The brain is a muscle, and the more you practice gratitude, the more you'll feel it.

Kerry Wekelo, COO of Actualize Consulting and author of Gratitude Infusion: Workplace Strategies for a Thriving Organizational Culture shares, in life, there are few things we know for certain. One of those is that we will face challenges and roadblocks—both literally and figuratively—as we navigate our daily life. We can be sailing along smoothly when BOOM, a challenge hits us out of the blue. How we navigate those challenges can make us stronger and more resilient. As the Dalai Lama said, "To remain indifferent to the challenges we face is indefensible. If the goal is noble, whether or not it is realized within our lifetime is largely irrelevant. What we must do therefore is to strive and persevere and never give up."

In fact, one of the leading researchers of gratitude, Robert A. Emmons, professor of psychology at the University of California, Davis actually suggests that we remember the bad things that happen to us because it is the contrast between good and bad times that makes us more appreciative of the good. He notes, "Consciously cultivating an attitude of gratitude builds up a sort of psychological immune system that can cushion us when we fall. There is scientific evidence that grateful people are more resilient to stress, whether minor everyday hassles or major personal upheavals. The contrast between suffering and redemption serves as the basis for one of my tips for practicing gratitude: remember the bad."

POSITIVE SCIENCE | 75

There are simple apps that help you record your gratitude. I love the one called *Five Minute Journal*. It's as simple as it sounds, and the ability to post a picture each day that reflects my gratitude.

The battle of the mind between positive and negative isn't always easy. But fortunately, there's science behind the process, and if you work on it, positive thinking will become much easier over time.

✓ Take Action

- ✓ Download the *Five Minute Journal* app (or any other one you like) and use it for the next 28 mornings straight.

- ✓ Right now, list the top three things you're grateful for in your life.

- ✓ Fill in the blank: What I love about myself is

_____

and

_____

"This book will provide you actionable steps to be your best self and encourage you to celebrate your successes. With personal stories and scientific data, you will want to make changes to enhance your life."

— **Kerry Alison Wekelo, COO of Actualize Consulting and author of Gratitude Infusion: Workplace Strategies for a Thriving Organizational Culture**

[8]

Brain Science

> **"Life is similar to golf, which is a game of inches. The most important are the six inches between your ears."**
>
> — Arnold Palmer, professional golfer with a career spanning over six decades, 62 PGA Tour titles, and 7 Major titles.

Arnold Palmer has a point. As difficult as it is widely known to get that little ball into that equally small hole in the game of golf, the G.O.A.T. (Greatest Of All Time) still thinks the real battle is in the mind.

We've talked about how positivity affects our ability to think through choices, and how gratitude and meditation are a part of a positive outlook. So, now let's dive more into meditation.

For years, I resisted meditation. I would hear about how important meditation is for clarifying your focus, being more positive, and finding creative solutions to life's challenges. Yet I just couldn't see myself sitting like a monk with my knees crossed, hands on knees, eyes closed, and perfectly still. I call this MSUing (Making Stuff Up). I was making up this story that it was impossible for me to meditate. But it wasn't really impossible. Eventually, after hearing about the benefits over and over again, I learned how to meditate. I discovered that you don't have to sit in any weird positions, and you can even keep your eyes open. I was able to do it, and my thoughts became so much clearer.

Meditation, for me, is the most radical thing a human can do. It a way to shift your mind to be more relaxed about what it's thinking. Most importantly, it allows you to be more prepared for the future and get clearer on where you need to take action. Meditation has really allowed me to focus on and go after the WIN: What's Important Now.

The Most Beautiful Waterfall

Here's the analogy that encouraged me to finally try meditation. Imagine the biggest and most beautiful waterfall you have ever seen. Your mind works very much like this beautiful waterfall. All the water falling over the ledge is your daily thoughts.

If you allow all that water to land on top of you, you won't be able to move. You'll be pinned down by the pressure.

Eventually, you'll drown. If you try to hold the waterfall back, you'll get pummeled. Bare hands can't stop the force of the water. However, if you allow those thoughts to pass through the pool instead of landing on you or trying to resist, you'll be free to move. You can even step aside and enjoy the beauty of water. Once you understand how to control—not eliminate—the flow of your thoughts, you can choose which ones to pay attention to. Free from pressure, you can decide what to take action on.

First, let's clarify what meditation *isn't*. Nancy Colier, author of *The Power of Off: The Mindful Way to Stay Sane in a Virtual World*, explained in a Psychology Today article that meditation is not about calming the mind—contrary to popular opinion. It will also not completely shut off your thinking.

She explains that the goal of meditation is not to *change* anything. On the contrary, you meditate to *observe*. It actually doesn't matter whether or not it quiets your mind. Sometimes your mind will quiet as a result, but that's not the goal of meditation.

Instead, meditation alters your relationship with your thoughts. In other words, you identify with them less. And when you stop identifying with them as much, you no longer see your thoughts as the end-all-be-all truth of the matter. When you stop paying them that attention, they sometimes scream even louder. And that's okay.

After a period of time spent meditating, you come to realize that you are not your thoughts, beliefs, or ideas. Colier said,

"Everything can change as a result of not trying to change anything." Instead, we are just a witness.

Awaken Your Mind

"The purpose of meditation is not to change our mind, but to awaken the self that is aware of it," continued Colier. So, as long as you just observe, you are doing it right. Just the act of meditation is doing it right.

We don't take enough time to do nothing. When we don't care for our minds, we get stressed. Being present in the moment is vital.

Being present means:

- not being lost in thought,
- not being distracted, and
- not being overwhelmed by difficult emotions.

In 2010, Harvard psychologists Matthew Killingsworth and Daniel Gilbert conducted a study with 2,250 individuals. They were shocked to discover that the participants all had wandering minds and were not fully engaged with what was right in front of them for a whopping 47 percent of the time.

Imagine what we could do with that time if we weren't so controlled by our thoughts. Imagine what this would do for our happiness level. As Killingsworth reported, "Mind-wandering is an excellent predictor of people's happiness. In fact, how often our minds leave the present is a better predictor of our happiness than the activities in which we're engaged."

Meditation brings you back to the present moment. It's a sort of focused relaxation. It allows you to extinguish the storylines in your mind and the things you tell yourself. The founder of Headspace, Andy Puddicombe said, "We can't change every little thing that happens to us, but we can change the way we experience it."

Here are some scientific benefits that most people will experience from meditation:

- Better sleep
- Fewer negative emotions
- More patience and tolerance
- A relaxed perspective on stressful situations
- Increased focus on the present
- Lower stress levels
- Stronger self-awareness
- More imagination and creativity

Champions Meditate

For a real-life example, successful athletes are notorious for using meditation to improve their game. The following champions are just a few who are known to meditate before or during games:

- **Michael Jordan** - Six National Basketball Finals champion and five-time Most Valuable Player.

- **Carli Lloyd** - Two-time soccer World Cup Champion and two time Gold Medal Champion.

- **Lebron James** - Played in eight consecutive National Basketball Finals with three different teams.

- **Derek Jeter** - Five World Series Baseball Championships and 14-time All-Star player.

- **Misty May-Treanor and Kerri Walsh** - Three-time Olympic Gold Medalists in Women's beach volleyball.

- **Tom Brady** - Seven-time football Super Bowl Champion and five-time Most Valuable Player.

- **Ginger Huber** - World Aquatics Champion in high diving.

- **Stephen Curry** - Six-time National Basketball All-Star and two-time Most Valuable Player.

You can find tools to help you meditate, too. I love a simple app that enables you to deal with different aspects of life, and there are several good ones out there for meditation. Two of my favorites are *Calm* and *Headspace*. Each one provides simple, thirty-day plans to help you learn to meditate. They also provide calming music and other guidance to help get you started.

Lebron James is with Calm and has a series of meditation techniques that you should try. Lebron shares some great stories about his meditation practice, including how he meditates on the bench before entering the game. Even my 13-year-old son, Riley, loves the Lebron James meditation techniques.

I'm certainly not saying meditation will be easy. Quite the contrary. When you get started, you may find that you're even more agitated by your restless mind than before. But again, there's really no wrong way to meditate. If you're doing it, you're doing it right. The important part is that you just do it.

Clear your schedule for ten minutes and find a quiet place to be still. Just breathe. Then observe your thoughts and see what you find. It will open up a whole new world for you and bring into perspective What's Important Now. Arnold Palmer couldn't be more correct that life is a game of inches, and "the most important are the six inches between your ears."

✓ Take Action

- ✓ Download a meditation app from your app store, Calm.com, or Headspace.com.

- ✓ Practice meditating for ten minutes every morning, for 28 days.

- ✓ Take note of which benefits you have experienced most from meditating.

    Notice if you experience better sleep, fewer negative emotions, more patience and tolerance, a relaxed perspective on stressful situations, increased focus on the present, lower stress levels, stronger self-awareness, or more imagination and creativity.

"With awareness, we can make conscious choices, instead of letting our habitual thoughts and patterns run the show."

— **Tamara Levitt, Head Instructor of Mindfulness at Calm**

[9]

Body Science

> "I hated every minute of training, but I said, don't quit. Suffer now and live the rest of your life as a champion."
>
> —Muhammad Ali, professional boxer, activist, and philanthropist nicknamed "The Greatest."

Our bodies are capable of phenomenal things. We've already talked about the power of our minds, but what about the power of our bodies? What are our bodies capable of when we focus and put them in motion?

First, let's discuss a study out of Finland that looked at how an active lifestyle affects you long term. There are many scientific things that happen when you exercise and move your body.

Our mitochondria (the powerhouse of our cells) are more efficient at burning fat when we're active. Exercise also lowers other damaging chemicals found that accumulate in those with obesity or who have diabetes.

Researchers believe the healthier the mitochondria, the more likely we will age better and not develop heart disease, diabetes, Alzheimer's, or Parkinson's disease. This is how exercise impacts our overall health in a positive way.

Scientists also found that exercise increases insulin sensitivity (thereby reducing the risk of type 2 diabetes), lowers cholesterol, improves our unsaturated to saturated fat ratio, and lowers the biomarkers of cardiovascular risk.

Exercise helps everyone, regardless of your age or current state of health. Dr. Susan Cheng, from Harvard-affiliated Brigham and Women's Hospital, says that people who have previously had a heart attack have a twenty percent less chance of developing more severe heart trouble if they do an aerobic exercise program—especially one focused on cardiovascular issues.

Exercise also leads to weight loss, reduced blood pressure, improved muscle strength and better sleep quality. It even puts you in a better mood and makes your mind sharper.

Exercise Should Be Fun, Not Too Strenuous

So, you're probably wondering, how long you need to exercise to get such great benefits. Dr. Cheng says it's ideal to get in thirty minutes of daily exercise. (Other experts say to shoot for at least three to four days a week.) What intensity is beneficial? Moderate is good. If the exercise is fun and not too strenuous, it's a good indicator that you're at a moderate level. I remember a time in my life when I wasn't that interested in exercising. I'd been an athlete since I was eight years old, and I just found myself getting lazy about it for no particular reason. I'm glad that happened because it taught me a lesson. I learned that when I stopped moving, I gained 34 pounds and felt horrible.

It got increasingly worse, until I finally took the hit and accepted responsibility for who I was becoming. I put myself back on a regular exercise routine which started with walking around the block. I quickly noticed I felt better. Then, I began jogging around the block, and today I love running miles with my headphones on. It allows me to cheat a little and indulge in some of my favorite meals. This alone is a great motivator to be able to eat what I want to eat.

Wendy Suzuki is a Professor of Neuroscience and Psychology at the New York University Center for Neural Science and popular science communicator. She became interested in the subject of exercise when she saw the benefits of it for herself as she was grant writing for a different research subject. Her observations inspired her to switch her studies altogether and focus on how exercise affects the brain.

Suzuki tells a story of being overwhelmed by her original research. She was working hard and doing little else. While she was studying something that interested her, she still found herself miserable and having no social life. One day though, she exercised and experienced an immediate mood and energy boost from the activity. Afterwards, when she sat down and started writing, she noticed she had more focus and her long-term memory was better than before. This piqued her interest greatly.

Suzuki found that exercise has an immediate, long-lasting, and protective effect on our brains. Our brains are complex, so she began to study why this was the case.

First of all, the brain is made up of several different areas. Two of those areas are the prefrontal cortex (which helps us make decisions, focus our attention, and hold our personality), and the hippocampus (which stores our long-term memory).

Through her research and personal experiences, Suzuki found that exercise was one of the most transformative actions we can participate in to affect these parts of our brains. She discovered that not only were the effects immediate, but after exercise, focus and attention improves for at least two hours. It will also improve reaction times.

Exercise Benefits

Here are some other things in the body that improve with exercise:

- Production of new brain cells in the hippocampus, which creates more volume and improves long-term memory.

- Increase in good-mood neurotransmitters, with long-lasting impact.
- Reduced chance of neurodegenerative diseases and aging effects.

We can see from Suzuki's research that our bodies gain some amazing benefits from exercise. When we focus, we can do some incredible things with our bodies. To blow your mind, here are a few astounding records that have been set. These records help me challenge myself when my mind says I can't do one more mile or another push up.

- **Push-ups**: 10,507 by Minoru Yoshida

- **Sit-ups:** 17,000 by Captain Wayne E. Rollings

- **Pull-ups:** 7,600 by John Orth

- **Most miles ran without stopping:** 350 miles by Dean Karnazes

Now, most of these numbers are not realistic for the average person. I'm not suggesting you attempt these kinds of repetitions, or even that you need to try! These statistics are just to blow your mind and show what's possible for some people when they exercise and focus their brains on one more repetition.

It's amazing what our bodies can do when we focus and take care of them. But remember, even thirty minutes of exercise a day at a moderate level is enough to make a significant improvement to your health.

Got Sleep?

Exercise also helps in getting a good night's sleep. As you improve your sleep, you're likely to see your nervous system better regulated, cognitive function improved, and your immune system strengthened. All of this works together to make your body strong and able to accomplish whatever you want during the day.

If you could only choose one thing, would it be food, water or sleep? As you may have guessed, I love science, so let's review the facts based on multiple medical studies.

- **Food**: Humans can live for more than 21 days without food.
- **Water**: If all the conditions are right, humans can survive up to 7 days without water.
- **Sleep**: Most humans cannot make it more than 3 days without sleep.

Yes, sleep is that important to the body. And let's face it, if you don't get sleep first, you won't be able to find the food and water that you need. Yet most people cheat themselves out of this valuable commodity. But sleep is within your control, and you can go to bed a little earlier to make sure you get the sleep you need.

How much sleep do we need? The National Sleep Foundation convened experts from sleep, anatomy, and physiology, as well as pediatrics, neurology, gerontology, and gynecology to reach a consensus from the broadest range of scientific disciplines. The panel revised the recommended sleep ranges for all six children and teenage groups. Here's a summary of the daily hours of sleep recommended (including naps):

- **Newborn** (0 to 3 months): 14 to 17 hours

- **Infant** (4 to 12 months): 12 to 16 hours

- **Toddler** (1 to 2 years): 11 to 14 hours

- **Preschool** (3 to 5 years): 10 to 13 hours

- **School Age** (6 to 12 years): 9 to 12 hours

- **Teen** (13 to 18 years): 8 to 10 hours

- **Adult** (18 to 65 years): 7 or more hours per night

- **Retired** (65 years and older): 8 to 9 hours

Following these guidelines, this means an 85-year-old person will have slept for more than 28 years. And all of that sleep will have been well worth it.

As you have witnessed, exercise has a profound effect on our bodies, and that is deeply rooted in many body systems. The good news is that much like meditation, getting out there and doing it is the important part. Don't focus on overdoing it with too many weights or too many miles; just get out there and move briskly for thirty minutes a day. Then watch how it affects your body and mind!

✓ Take Action

- ✓ What exercises do you love to do? (Not like, but *love*.) Add fifteen minutes to your daily calendar to do this exercise, preferably in the morning when there are fewer distractions than later in the day.

- ✓ Are you getting the recommended number of hours of sleep for you? If not, note down the time you need to go to bed to get the minimum hours in every night.

- ✓ Tell someone you know that can hold you accountable. Tell them your exercise routine and sleep schedule. Make sure you keep it fun, so you don't burn yourself out.

♥

"Hernani shares his passion in Sports, Science, and Meditation in this book. A compelling read with simple concepts that get to the point, real life stories and insightful tools. Becoming a Champion is within reach!"

— **Mabel Lun, NextGEN, PRIDE Industries**

♥

[10]

Acts of Kindness

> "The most important thing is to try and inspire people so that they can be great in whatever they want to do."
>
> —Kobe Bryant, five-time National Basketball Champion and 18-time All-Star player.

We all know it's kind of fun to buy things. But there are scientific reasons why giving is even more rewarding to our human nature than getting stuff.

Giving comes in many forms, from giving gifts to donating money to charity, to volunteering your personal time. Jason Marsh and Jill Suttie wrote an article for Greater Good Magazine entitled *5 Ways Giving Is Good*. Let's look at those five ways.

1. Happiness

A 2008 Harvard Business School study by Michael Norton and his partners revealed that giving money to others made people happier than buying things for themselves.

In a similar study, happiness expert Sonja Lyubomirsky, professor at the University of California, Riverside, found similar results when she had people do five kind acts each week for six consecutive weeks. Participants were happier than when they weren't doing kind acts.

A 2006 National Institute of Health study by Jorge Moll discovered that when people donate to charity, it activates the regions of the brain associated with trust, social connection, and pleasure. It's believed that "altruistic behavior releases endorphins in the brain," producing the positive feeling known as "helper's high."

2. Health

Stephen Post's book, *Why Good Things Happen to Good People,* explains that giving to others has a positive impact on our health. Even elderly people who pitch in to help their relatives and neighbors are up to 44 percent less likely to die than their counterparts who are not actively helping others. This is according to one study from the University of California, Berkeley, and another from the University of Michigan.

It's believed that giving to others lowers your own stress. And the lower your stress, the lower your blood pressure, and the fewer detrimental effects impact your body.

3. Connectedness and Cooperation

When we give, we usually get something back. These exchanges "promote a sense of trust and cooperation that strengthens our ties to others," said John Cacioppo, author of *Loneliness: Human Nature and the Need for Social Connection*. He also found that the more we reciprocate altruism, the happier and more successful we are.

Giving and receiving brings us closer together. It creates a healthy sense of interdependence.

4. Gratitude

Here's that popular word again that we explored in chapter six. We're returning to gratitude because it helps transform lives. Many studies have found that gratitude is a key to our happiness. One study out of Florida State University showed that "expressing gratitude to a close friend or romantic partner strengthens our sense of connection to that person."

Happiness researcher Barbara Fredrickson believes words and actions of gratitude "boost our own positivity" and affect others the same.

5. Inspiration

Giving inspires others to do the same. Scientists have found that giving releases oxytocin, which is a hormone that produces feelings of euphoria and connection. These chemicals are a part of why we give. Through these feelings, we inspire others to give as well, and we can affect hundreds to thousands of people who might notice the generous acts in turn.

When I started thinking more about giving, these concepts made sense. For example, when I shop, it's not uncommon for me to want to pick up an item that I know a friend will love. I almost have to keep myself from doing it. People are notorious for saying, "You didn't have to do that." But I enjoy picking out and giving gifts so much that I couldn't resist. Now, I know that I'm hard-wired chemically to want to give to others. It probably makes me feel better than they do when they receive what I bought for them!

Elizabeth Dun, Professor and Happiness Researcher at the University of British Columbia, in BC, Canada, gave a Ted Talk about generosity and giving. She had an extra insight into the action of giving.

She performed an exercise where she gave toddlers a bowl of goldfish crackers. This made the toddlers very happy. But what made the toddlers even happier was when they gave some of these crackers away to other people.

This got Dunn thinking about how the act of giving makes us happy. She proceeded on a journey of helping others, which taught her how people experienced the positivity of giving when they felt a connection to the people they were helping and could easily see how their generosity impacted their lives.

For example, Dunn got involved with the Group of Five. This was a program where any five Canadians could get together and sponsor a group of Syrian refugees. She proceeded to pull together not only five people, but over twenty, and brought a family to Canada from Syria. The group was elated to see how their money and efforts brought a new quality of life to this family, and they were propelled to stay involved in the family's lives after their arrival in Canada.

Dunn also mentioned the program Plenty of Plates. This service offers three-course meals to homeless people in their area. They're sponsored every night by a different local business, whose employees also make and serve the meals. The community all benefits from these efforts. Dunn said that we need to give "to appreciate our shared humanity," and Plenty of Plates is a prime example of how this can operate.

The bottom line is that it matters not only that we give, but *how* we give. We need to stop thinking of giving as an obligation but rather as a source of pleasure. Just giving money isn't enough to elicit a positive response. We need to see how our money will make a difference in the recipients' life.

When You Can't Afford to Give Back

You may feel you're not in a position to help anyone else right now. You might have a challenging situation in your life that doesn't allow you to offer financial assistance. It might feel like giving back is the last thing you should be concerned with right now.

But here's the hard truth: You will always have an excuse not to help and the ability to overcome those excuses. We all have money, time, or talent to give at one point or another. If you don't have money to give, you can always share your time or your talents. If you've been creative with your brainstorming, you'll have found manageable ways to give back to your community without jeopardizing your productivity or resources.

In fact, the sooner you start giving back, the faster you'll feel the five feelings we discussed above: happiness, health, connection and cooperation, gratitude, and inspiration. The more you give, the more you receive. I've seen this play out time and time again. It's the classic chicken and egg situation; you can wait to improve your life before giving back, or you can give back and improve your life. It's proven that the latter is infinitely better.

If you're looking for some ideas, here are 12 places where you can give back:

1. Give your time, attention, or resources to your own family. Consider those who are elderly, ill, or just need some positive reinforcement.
2. Volunteer or provide for your local schools.
3. Have a garage sale and donate the proceeds to charity.
4. Spend time in a senior center talking with elderly citizens.
5. Coach a youth team.
6. Tutor a local student.
7. Serve meals at local shelters.
8. Join a community board.
9. Volunteer to be a guide.
10. Help your neighbor right next door.
11. Join a food co-operative.
12. Become a hospital volunteer.

Here are some great organizations that I have been a part of in helping others:

- Rotary International: Rotary.org

- Kiwanis International: Kiwanis.org

- American Red Cross: RedCross.org

- Salvation Army: SalvationArmyUSA.org

- Society for the Prevention of Cruelty to Animals: Aspca.org

- Ticket To Dream for Foster Kids: Tickettodream.org/

Ticket to Dream, the organization helping foster kids, is particularly close to my heart. When I first heard about how foster kids are thrown into the system, I knew it was a bad situation. The stories tore at my heart. I recall a three-year-old girl and her five-year-old brother who were found by authorities in the backseat of a car. Both their parents had died overdosing on drugs in the front seat. As if that wasn't bad enough, when the kids entered the foster care system, they were separated. They only saw each other at summer camp. It wasn't these kids' fault for what happened to them.

My children are wonderful, but parenting even the best kids can be a challenge at times. Foster parents have kids who've been through intense trauma, and they take on all the messiness that comes with that. They need our support. I'm so thankful for our foster care system, and we can do more to help.

I learned while working with the Ticket to Dream Foundation that, "Not everyone can be a foster parent, but anyone can help a foster child." We need to give back, and we need to hold ourselves accountable for doing so.

If you don't find the right fit the first time, keep trying until you both benefit from your generous time and efforts. The worst thing you can do is *nothing*.

✓ Take Action

- ✓ Decide what you can give at this time. Is it time, money, or both? I always recommend starting with time and investing in the organization that you passionately want to help most.

- ✓ Decide which charity your company will support and how you'll start giving back. Visit one of the non-profit organization websites above and call your local organization to get involved.

- ✓ Email me at Hernani@BalancedIQ.com and tell me how you going to give back. I read every email, and we can hold each other accountable.

Reviews from awesome people like you help others to feel confident about reading this book.

Please take a moment to leave a quick review on where you bought this book.

[11]

Celebrate your Success

> "Isn't life about determining your own finish line? The journey has always been about reaching your own other shore, no matter what it is, and the dream continues."
>
> —Diana Nyad, legendary swimmer who, at the age of 62, became the first person to swim from Cuba to Florida without the aid of a shark cage, swimming 111 miles in 53 hours from Havana to Key West.

Even though it's been nearly twenty years now, I can still remember how frightened I was during my daughter, Carmina's, birth. Arriving at the hospital, we expected everything to be pretty routine. We checked in and got my wife, Angie's, vitals. Then the hospital staff did an ultrasound, and that's where everything changed. They couldn't find a heartbeat.

The nurse called in the doctor, who couldn't see any sign of life, either. Just nine months earlier, we'd sat in that same hospital and listened as the ultrasound picked up Carmina's heart beating strong and steady and filling us with joy. That's was when it really clicked: I was going to be a dad. Now... we thought she'd be stillborn.

After twelve emotionally and physically painful hours of labor, Angie gave birth to Carmina. She was alive and we were elated! But still, something wasn't right.

At first, the baby didn't cry. Then she suddenly screamed and turned blue. The doctors grabbed her from my arms and started working on her. They were able to revive her, but for a while, she was very unstable. But ultimately, our daughter is a fighter. She's a champion and today she's a strong and intelligent teenager.

My wife is a champion too. She labored twelve hours of birth not knowing if she would give birth to a baby that was alive and breathing. It was all so much for both my daughter and wife to overcome. But they pushed through, and four years later, our son, Riley, joined our family. (In a much less eventful birth, thankfully!)

Life Is Full of Hurdles, Not Walls.

There are hurdles for everyone to overcome in life. We've covered many different strategies for how to come out a winner. The first thing to start with is W-I-N. What's Important Now? Look at your situation and think about the next logical step you can take. Did you just get a scary diagnosis? Research the closest expert and make an appointment. Order a book about the condition and start reading and taking notes for your appointment. Call a close friend and confide how you're feeling. Join a support group with others that have a similar diagnosis. Just keep making the next best choice each hour, each minute, according to what's most important now.

Doing nothing should never be an option.

We talked about having a Fixed versus a Growth Mindset. Take the example of getting a scary diagnosis. A Fixed Mindset may think, *Well, that's it. I have this disease now and there's nothing I can do about it.* A Growth Mindset considers what is within control, and makes changes accordingly. A Growth Mindset looks at a negative situation and considers what can be learned and how it can come out even healthier on the other side.

Doing nothing should never be an option.

We also talked about positivity. When you remain positive and focus on what's possible, your brain allows you to consider more options. The minute you focus on the negative, you stop seeing all of the different possibilities. It's literally how our brains work.

Doing nothing should never be an option.

It's also important to celebrate small victories. I remember teaching my children how to golf. I would take them to the driving range with me to hit balls. Golf is a notoriously difficult sport to learn and master, so imagine the challenge it presents for a child. When I was first teaching Carmina, when she was eight-years-old, I was too tough on her. I guess I wanted to raise a golf prodigy, and in my eagerness, I criticized her too much. I thought I was doing the right thing, but she hated the sport because of it.

When I figured out it was better to praise any small accomplishment, like just making contact with the ball, she started to enjoy playing and eventually became one of the best golfers in her high school league. I did the same with Riley, and both my kids enjoy the sport today.

This really taught me the importance of celebrating small victories. Celebrate the positive. When I criticized too much, Carmina shut down and couldn't see anything good about playing. When I was more positive, she opened up. There's definitely a lesson there for us all.

This kind of strategy also works great if you have a huge goal in mind, like losing seventy pounds or paying off $50,000 in credit card debt. These are the kinds of goals that are not met overnight. Trying to get to the finish line can be arduous and discouraging. One way to tackle how you'll inevitably feel along the way is by celebrating the small wins. Treat yourself to an outing or something new (within your budget) every time you lose five or ten pounds. Each time you pay off a credit card, have some friends over for drinks and celebrate with a mini credit card-themed party. Do something you enjoy that feels like a treat and acknowledges your accomplishment.

Doing nothing should never be an option.

One More Thing

There's one more thing I'd like for you to do. Please sit down and write a letter to yourself as though three months have already passed and you've focused on the proven strategies of this book. Write what you want to accomplish as though you've already met your goals.

Here's how to write it:

1. Think about what you want to accomplish and why it's important to you.

2. Pick the top three things that you're confident you can accomplish in ninety days.

3. Write the letter to yourself. Talk about who you are now, after those ninety days, and where you find yourself.

4. Be casual and talk about yourself in the first person. (Refer to yourself as "I.")

5. Summarize your key values and what you believe in.

6. List out and commit to the top five things you took away from this book.

7. Place a reminder in your calendar three months from now to read your letter!

For example, the letter could start out:

Dear Hernani,

Great job on meeting your goal of doing What's Important Now! I'm so proud that you kept up with running three miles four times a week, participated in the half marathon, and lost 10 pounds....

Why do you write this letter three months into the future? Because ninety days is a good amount of time for some of these new concepts to stick and make a difference in your life.

Having a positive outlook that you'll meet these goals and speaking them into reality is a great place to end our time together. Thank you for taking the time to read this book, and I wish you success in all of your endeavors.

Doing nothing should never be an option.

✓ Take Action

- ✓ Write your letter now. Keep it simple and don't push it to a later date to complete.

- ✓ Email me at Hernani@BalancedIQ.com and tell me the top five things you liked about this book. Feedback is a gift, and I would love to hear from you. Yes, I do read every email!

- ✓ Who's the most important person in your life? **Yes, you are!** Go do what you've always wanted to do and I'll always be by your side!

Remember Frank DeAngelis quote: "People don't care how much you know until they know how much you care."

Write down three people to give a copy of this book to:

1) _____

2) _____

3) _____

Many thanks for honoring me with your valuable time. Don't hesitate to reach out any time.

With Love ♥ & Gratitude,

About the author

Hernani Alves is an entrepreneur, author, and international speaker, with over twenty years of experience as a sales executive for a $3 billion company. He's the founder of Balanced IQ, a company that helps leaders build world-class teams and to get the results they desire. Hernani resides in California.

Learn more: HernaniAlves.com

Email: Hernani@BalancedIQ.com

Speaker and Consultant

Hernani has been invited to deliver keynotes and training programs all over the world. His clients include well-known brands like Stanford University, University of California, Oklahoma University, HR.com, Recruiter, Idea Mensch, CEO World Magazine, Conscious Company, The Revolution, Extreme Leadership, and more.

Hernani is a skilled presenter and trainer. The audience will walk away with something real, something dynamic, and something that transforms their lives for the better.

To book Hernani as a speaker for live events, podcasts, online summits, or conferences,
please contact him directly: Hernani@BalancedIQ.com

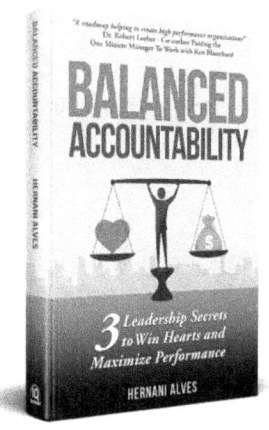

He is also the author of the best selling book:

Balanced Accountability

Available anywhere you buy books: Amazon, Wal-Mart, Target, Apple and more.

Balanced Accountability: How to Win Hearts to Maximize Performance

"Hernani's work on Balanced Accountability drives every aspect of an organization's success. Here is a roadmap helping to create high performance organizations.
—**Dr. Robert L Lorber,** CEO of The Lorber Kamai Consulting Group, Co-author *Putting The One Minute Manager To Work* with Ken Blanchard

"Balanced Accountability should be required reading for every manager and entrepreneur."
—**Steve Farber, Founder**, The Extreme Leadership Institute; author, The Radical LEAP, Greater Than Yourself, and Love Is Just Damn Good Business

Resources

Alves, Hernani. *Balanced Accountability.* (Roseville: Balanced IQ, 2019)

Anchor, Shawn. *The Happiness Advantage.* (New York: Currency 2010)

Andal, Elizabeth. *Famous Failures to Success.* (London: Lifehack, 2019)

Barnes, Jamie. *The Importance of Sleep.* (Ascot, Australia: ESSA, 2015)

Cacioppo, John. *Loneliness: Human Nature and the Need for Social Connection.* (New York: Norton & Company, 2008)

Cheng, Susan. *The Science of Exercise Shows Benefits Beyond Weight Loss.* (Boston: Harvard Medical School, 2013)

Clear, James. *The Science of Positive Thinking.* (New York: Huff Post, 2017)

Colier, Nancy. *The Power of Off: The Mindful Way to Stay Sane in a Virtual World?* (New York: Psychology Today, 2013)

Dunn, Elizabeth. *Helping Others Makes us Happier.* (Vancouver, Canada: University of British Columbia, 2019)

Dweck, Carol. *Mindset: The New Psychology of Success.* (New York: Ballantine Books, 2017)

Emmons, R.A. *How Gratitude Can Help You Through Hard Times.* (Berkeley, California, Great Good Magazine 2013)

Fredrickson, Barbara. *Love 2.0.* (Victoria, Australia: Penguin Group, 2013)

Gallup. *2019 Global Emotions Report*. (Washington D.C: https://www.gallup.com/analytics/248906/gallup-global-emotions-report-2019.aspx, 2019)

Grant, Heidi. *Do You Play to Win—or to Not Lose?* (Boston: Harvard Business Review, 2013)

Killingsworth, Matthew. *Track your Happiness.* (Boston: Harvard University, 2013)

Ledgerwood, Alison. *Simple Trick to Improve Positive Thinking.* (Davis: University of California, Davis, 2013)

Lewis, Michael. *Ways to Volunteer Your Time and Give Back to the Community.* (Portland: Money Crashers, 2017)

Marsch, Jason. *Ways Giving is Good for You.* (Berkeley: Greater Good Magazine, 2010)

MBA Rendezvous. *Nelson Mandela.* (India: MBA Rendezvous, 2014)

Minority Mindset Team. *Rags to Riches.* (Ann Harbor: https://theminoritymindset.com/rags-riches-inspirational-success-stories/, 2017)

Norton, Michael. *Money spent on others can buy happiness.* (Boston: Harvard Business School, 2008)

Post, Stephen. *Why Good Things Happen to Good People.* (New York, Random House, 2007)

Puddicombe, Andy. *All it takes is 10 Mindful Minutes.* (New York: TED Talk, 2018)

Schnurr, Lisa. *Scientific Studies That Prove the Power of Positive Thinking.* (New York: Medium, 2019)

Selking, Amber. *Dare to Think Like a Champion Today.* (Southbend: TEDX, 2018)

St. John, Richard. *8 Traits Successful People Have in Common: 8 to be Great.* (Toronto: Train of Thought Arts, 2010)

Stillman, Jessica. *Gratitude Physically Changes Your Brain.* (Des Moines, Inc.: 2016)

Suzuki, Wendy. *The Brain Changing Benefits of Exercise.* (New York. Center of Neural Science: 2017)

Wekelo, Kerry. *Gratitude Infusion: Workplace Strategies for a Thriving Organizational Culture.* (Virginia. Actualize Consulting: 2020)

Willis, Brian. *WINx.* (Providence: The Virtus Group, 2015

www.ingramcontent.com/pod-product-compliance
Lightning Source LLC
Chambersburg PA
CBHW070954080526
44587CB00015B/2302